# A LIFE WORTH
# DEFENDING

EJ OWENS

# A LIFE WORTH DEFENDING

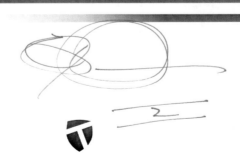

TATE PUBLISHING
AND ENTERPRISES, LLC

Published by Tate Publishing & Enterprises, LLC
127 E. Trade Center Terrace | Mustang, Oklahoma 73064 USA
1.888.361.9473 | www.tatepublishing.com

Tate Publishing is committed to excellence in the publishing industry. The company reflects the philosophy established by the founders, based on Psalm 68:11,
*"The Lord gave the word and great was the company of those who published it."*

Book design copyright © 2015 by Tate Publishing, LLC. All rights reserved.
*Cover design by Junriel Boquecosa*
*Interior design by Jimmy Sevilleno*

Published in the United States of America

ISBN: 978-1-68028-440-9
Sports & Recreation / Shooting
14.11.21

To the love of my life, Jennifer
You are my inspiration and my rock!
My children—Kaleb, Olivia, and Ethan
You have made me proud
Daddy loves you…always and forever!
To my Lord and Savior Jesus Christ

Yea, though I walk through the valley of the
shadow of death, I will fear no evil.

(Ps 23:4)

# CONTENTS

# OPENING

Live your life with purpose, meaning and influence so that when the time arrives that you must defend it...it's a life worth defending.

**I FIND IT** a pleasure and a blessing that I can share these words with you. I have many instances in my life where I have contemplated my existence and purpose, as well as many that have blessed me when I haven't deserved it. These experiences, coupled with a multitude of influences and mentors, have helped shape my platform and resolve. I desire to live a life worth defending. It is a lifestyle and a mindset that I am constantly trying to perfect. I pray the following chapters serve as evidence to that. No matter where you are in your life, these next chapters are sure to help you solidify what you may already know about yourself and, more importantly, help you discover some things you many not knew existed in your pursuit to live a life worth defending.

As the protector of my family, loving father, responsible gun owner, and man of faith, I have a deep understanding of what these responsibilities might ask of me, and I want to share them with you. For that reason I write this book—to provide you an insight as to what I believe I must do each and every day to live a life worth defending until my time on earth is complete. We interact with so many people on a day-to-day basis and all too often we fail to see the influence we have and how, whether positive or negative, it affects others. I want you to realize that our time here is short and we must be about our business of making our loved ones, others, and ourselves better.

I carry a firearm everyday to protect myself and the ones I love. Some have said that carrying a gun is an ego boost and demonstrates a desire to shoot someone. I will tell you that I carry because I'm not finished living. I have things to do with my family, loved ones to share with, and a daughter to walk down the aisle. I am determined to prevent some oxygen thief from robbing me of those opportunities. It is important to point out that most bad guys will fire back, an experience we don't feel at our local gun range, and we must delve further in the understanding to the real potential that in the defense of our life, we may lose it. I would ask you to consider this: Are you living a life worth defending? Have you expressed your love to those that you do? Have you told your kids how much they really mean to you? Have you extended that hand of reconciliation to those who have offended you and to those you have offended? Have you lived your life with passion and commitment? Maybe you have…to a degree.

At the end I pray that you have no regrets and that you have lived life to the fullest, with purpose and meaning. Consider the teachings, influence, and meaning you have brought to others. As we go through this journey called life, remember that you take nothing with you when you leave and tomorrow is not promised. Remember this is the only ride we get so make the most of it. If you can't say for sure you have been *living* life, not existing, but truly *living*, it's time to start!

What lies behind us and what lies before us are tiny matters compared to what lies within us.

—Ralph Waldo Emerson

# 1

# BROKEN

Definition:

**bro·ken \\\'brō-kən\\**

*adjective*

: separated into parts or pieces by being hit, damaged, etc.
: not complete or full

IF I HAD some time to think hard on it, I might be able to remember those positive and encouraging things that others have bestowed upon me throughout my life. As with the opposite, it only takes a second to recall. Why is that? Generally, we are a negative society. What gets the headlines of the news? It is the horrific and gripping details of the atrocities that happened in our communities. Look at reality shows. We watch to see others mess up relationships, business opportunities, or just to see how screwed up that TV person is in general. We are attracted to others' inabilities and failures. Conversely, it grabs the attention of others when you screw up. When you do, there are certainly more than enough of your "friends" to help you in realizing it.

> We don't learn anything unless it's associated with a significantly emotional, traumatic event.–
>
> —U.S. Army Drill Sergeant (unknown)

Over time, these pointed-out failures and mistakes build on each other and develop a common theme. How can you be of worth when you keep failing? Well, I would like to point out that the ones doing the finger pointing have probably done the same thing and like to see, much like why we watch reality TV, others failing so they can make themselves feel better. I have certainly done my fair share of failing, whether jobs, relationships, and military, to include failing myself. Since I don't know you and you don't know me, we can't really relate to each other's individual failures, but we do have one very important thing in common—we are human and thus imperfect!

As humans, we have the innate capacity to think and process logic and other sensory information in order to put together plans and develop plausible answers to every situation we encounter. In the information gathering process, we identify the problem, identify the alternatives, and then evaluate the alternatives prior to making the decision. When the said problem affects us as an individual, we tend to prioritize our responses based on two things—*what it means to me* and *how does it affect me*. Let me share with you how this works at a very elementary level. As a child I would prioritize my parents' directions *around* my personal wants and activities. For example, my mother would tell me to bring down my dirty clothes so she could wash them. I would often head back to my room and return to the TV show I was watching, all along knowing that I should be doing what she told me to do. I didn't want to, plain and simple. I wanted to finish watching my show. That was what was important to me at the time, not her direction. In my mind she could wait, I had to finish what I was doing first. Even as adults we often find ourselves doing what we want to do and not necessarily what is the right thing to do—unless the two are mutually beneficial.

As adults, when we make decisions in life, they have ramifications, both positive and negative. As a child our parents would work to correct or even contain the amount of negative impact our poor decisions had on us, but as adults, well, no one is coming to rescue you. This is the harsh reality that adulthood has laying in wait for us. Just as I did to my parents, my children do the same thing to my wife and me so I can say with certainty that it is because we are truly selfish in nature. I am as guilty as the next when it comes to this, I assure you. There have been bad decisions made and tough consequences felt in my life that have caused me to stand alone and even get rejected by others. Yet, looking back on them, I am grateful for the experiences. Remember what I said in the beginning? "We don't learn anything unless it's associated with a significantly emotional, traumatic event." Well, I learned them with a price. Until these lessons are learned, we are bound to stand broken.

Brokenness, as in a state of emotion, is further defined by Merriam-Webster dictionary as subdued, humbled, contrite. I have certainly been all three. Because of my selfish actions, I have lost loved ones that I never expressed my true and complete feelings for. Because of my self-centered emotions, I have made poor business decisions that have led to lost opportunities, and

I have acted out on those emotions that hurt others. These events have hurt and even devastated me and I can honestly point out the problem to you—me! I was at the center of all of them. I have experienced the loss of friendships with friends and family. With the latter, it was usually because I wouldn't go with a train of thought or actions that, in the moment, seemed wrong to me but in the end proved to the right choice. On the other hand, I have had close friends and family who have hurt me with their words, their actions, and even their inactions.

Thanks to a *great* (sarcasm) public education environment, I have met people from vast economic, religious, and racial backgrounds. Suffice to say, I didn't get along with all of them, and it was not because of where they came from or their current "social status." It was because of our moral and ethical disagreements. I have been called every name in the book! Even though I knew I was right not to conform, I still found myself emotionally broken.

In my brokenness I became ineffective with my purpose, influence, and meaning. I slowly became callous and empty. I wandered around dwelling in my self-induced self-pity.

How could they say that about *me?*
How could they treat *me* like that?

It hurt! I was alone! My emotional state caused me to miss out on some very pivotal moments in the lives of my friends and family. Even though I might have been there in the physical aspect, emotionally I was absent. This brokenness was binding my emotions by clinging to my own personal will. My will, what I wanted, how I thought I ought to be treated, bound me to a fence post called selfishness. Out of that emotion I became angry and wanted others to hurt like I was. Therefore I was short with my temper and quick with anger. I was out of control. Let me share with you a little story to explain this point better.

When I was three my dad left my two-year-old sister, my newborn brother, and me. My mother was forced to go on welfare and had a tough time balancing work and taking care of three children, the children my dad said he had always wanted. My grandmother and grandfather graciously took care of me to help out Mom. What began as a little help grew into a regular routine. This routine lasted till I graduated high school. Over time, I called my grandmother "Mom" too. My grandparents raised me, with the help of my mother, until my last year of high school.

When I was seventeen and a cocky senior in high school, my grandmother (a school teacher) taught at my high school. Now, hold up a minute and think about it. My grandmother is teaching at my school and *I'm a senior*! Needless to say, her gazing eyes and all-knowing teacher friends tempered my "swagger," but I digress.

I can remember this story that I'm about to tell you like it happened yesterday. I walked out of the school and into the parking lot. My grandfather was there sitting in a blue minivan on the front row of parking spaces waiting to pick up my grandmother from school. It was December 1993 at Hernando High School in Hernando, Mississippi. It was a bright and sunny afternoon. I remember that it was a little brisk for that time of year in Mississippi. School had just let out for the weekend. I walked out to my car to get my baseball bag because I had practice after school. As I walked out to get my stuff from my car, I saw him and he waved. I waved back but didn't go say anything to him (here is where my selfishness still haunts me to this day) because I knew he would tell me to go home after practice. The baseball team was going to hang out after practice and I wanted to stay. So I didn't go over to him and say "Hi" because I wanted to hang out with the guys. As I grabbed my bag I gave him a look and a head nod and he smiled back at me with a slight wave of his hand. He picked up my grandmother and left for a Christmas vacation in Destin, Florida. I never saw him again...

While walking down the beautiful white sand beach of Destin, Florida, Dr. Ernest S. Owens sat down for a moment, clutched his chest, and laid back, never to wake up on this Earth again. He died in one of the most beautiful ways I can imagine. I'm thirty-seven at the time of this book and I still tear up at the thought of my selfishness and what it robbed me of. This was an epic life-changing event that was both emotional and traumatic. As you might imagine, that moment has stuck with me for quite a long time. I was angry with myself, angry at

God for taking him, and angry at the world, therefore unpleasant to be around. I lost some very close friends and even my girlfriend because I was consumed with being broken. Somewhere along the way, many years later, I forgave myself for that and committed to telling my family and friends how much they mean to me like it is the last time they may ever hear it.

There are plenty of other examples but I believe this one makes my point pretty clear. I finally came to the realization that I was indeed in control of my emotions. When I chose to take back control of those feelings and emotions, I started the healing process. I give them their due respect and processed them, and only then was I finally able put them away. It is so much easier to talk about it now then it was to actually doing it then. Remember, I said it took years to understand and forgive myself.

I have always had a very outgoing personality and that has both helped and hindered me throughout the years. During my senior year of high school, I was voted most likely to succeed, class clown, head of the morning announcement on the school TV network, contributor to the yearbook, was on the governing council for Future Business Leaders of America at school, lettered in baseball as a starting left-handed pitcher, and even runner up for homecoming king (like that really matters) but I failed to tell you that this was my only year at that school. Not bad for the "new" guy. I also had several in-school detentions for fighting too. Again, both a help and a hindrance!

After my grandfather died, I began to recall things that he used to say to me (interesting how that happens). Of them all, he used to tell me that I had a great head on my shoulders and could do anything I put my mind too, but if I didn't get my attitude in check, I was going to be in jail pretty quick. As a former Army Air Corps B-24 pilot, he had strongly suggested I go into the military. "Yeah, right! Not me!" That was not for me. I signed up a month after he passed on a delayed entry program.

After high school I went to a community college and studied Prehospital Emergency Medicine (Paramedic). After my first semester I went off to Army basic training and AIT (Advanced Individual Training) as a Combat Medic 91-W. It was there I was introduced to the concept of perseverance. Now not everybody needs to learn perseverance in the face of brokenness by going to the military, but I'm a hardheaded individual who requires a stiff kick in the rear, or two. I can tell you now that the old man was right (funny how hindsight is always twenty-twenty). This began my trial by fire in understanding that I am as a man and as a protector/provider. As dealing with brokenness goes, this was only the beginning.

Far too often, when we are broken, we become consumed by it. As you have read, I certainly was. It was more than grieving for a lost parent. It was more than dealing with the emotions surrounding the finality of death. It was a conscious act that had repercussions, and in this case, lasting negative repercussions. During that time, I allowed my purpose, meaning, and influence to become distorted and callous. In a sense, the chains of yesterday surrounded me and thus kept me awake many a night.

I'm sure you have had events in your life that have pulled you in omnidirectional paths where you have found yourself with nothing left to give. You have felt lost and lonely. You have felt like you were drowning in guilt and abandoned by it. Maybe you've lost a job because of it. Maybe you have had a failed marriage. I'm sure you've not realized a dream or two of yours. I'm even surer that you've lost your self-perspective at times. We all have. But you can change how that affects you! You are in control of your emotions and feelings and you can change them to be positive. I did!

We can't change our past but we can affect our present and future. You must first recognize that it actually happened. For all it's worth, both good and bad, it happened. Next, you must accept the sadness and heartache for what it is. These are emotions that you can't suppress because they tend to get bigger and worse as time goes on. I can tell you that the man in the mirror is the hardest man to please. Once we get them out in the open, we can deal with them for what they are not what we make them out to be. We can then see what the truth looks like. Many times the truth is drowned out by the emotional storm we are in.

In my own life, I can tell you that I have felt like I was one mistake away from being left this way. That is simply not the truth. The truth is we can forgive and we can move on. As with any traumatic event, including the death of a loved one, our resolve should not be to "get over it." You will never get over it! Our resolve should be to accept it and learn to deal with it. Let this moment be a part of your life, but not define you as a friend, parent, and a provider/protector. Give it its due but recognize it and deal with it emotionally, mentally, and spiritually till you can forgive others and yourself. Guilt has an awful way of reminding us of our faults.

In brokenness there is healing.

Find someone you can talk to, someone who can listen without judgment and condemnation. For me there is only one who can do both. I lean on my religious understanding to help shape and guide me. From one scared hand to the other, my Lord and Savior, Jesus Christ, accepts my faults, my doubts, and my brokenness. I have many more faults to discuss with him but with these that I have mentioned he has forgiven me. If you are not religious, I find not fault in you. This is simply my way of moving past brokenness and shaping the man and the life I deem worth defending. If we are broken then we have a binding we can't shake off. If the time comes that I must give my life for the ones I love, I pray I can do it with a clear conscience and an open heart. Should I meet my end during the encounter then so be it. I have worked to release myself of my brokenness and through it feel as if I can move without regret or doubt during my encounter.

It takes boldness to ask for favor despite your mistakes. You may fall, but you are not destroyed. I pray you live with boldness not brokenness. If you are not happy with the person you are right now, start today to make that change.

Forgiving does not erase the bitter past. A healed memory is not a deleted memory. Instead, forgiving what we cannot forget creates a new way to remember. We change the memory of our past into a hope for our future.

—Lewis B. Smedes, Author

# 2

# HOME

Definition:

**home \ˈhōm\**

*noun*

: the place where a person lives

: a family living together in one building, house, etc.
: a place where something normally or naturally lives
or is located

WE ALL HAVE our version of what home is. To some it's
a certain house, a bedroom, possibly a living room with
a fully lit Christmas tree. To others it may be the smell
of Dad's biscuits and gravy on a cold winter's morning or Mom's fried chicken on Sunday afternoon. The
word *home* is synonymous with childhood for most. As
for me, home is…my grandparents sitting in the living
room watching TV while I try not to get caught out
of bed peeking at them. To some, home represents an
environment that they try hard never to recreate with
their children. All the same, it is home. We are not so
fortunate as to be able to pick neither our family nor
the environment that we were raised in. However, there
comes a point when we leave home and break out on our
own. It's funny to me because I tried so hard to leave as
a new adult only to get out on my own and long to be
back under their roof. I can remember my first apartment. I was eighteen and a freshman in collage with a
two-bedroom apartment. I got several boxes of dishes
and kitchen supplies from Mom's cabinets that would
never be missed and stacked them with pride on my bare
shelves. Boy, did I think this was living the life…until
my head hit the pillow that first night. It was quiet.

It was in that quiet that I learned how much my
grandparents and Mom had actually done for me. There
wasn't the mumbling in the kitchen or the slapping of
dishes being put up from the dishwasher. There wasn't
the faint noise of the evening news echoing from the
living room or my grandmother telling my grandfather

to be quiet because "EJ is trying to sleep." No…it was just quiet. Our parents play a strong part in shaping us for success—or, in some cases, failure—in the big world. For me I was lucky to have great parents who, in my own opinion at seventeen, didn't know anything (don't act like you didn't feel the same at that age). I was ready, just let me go and I'll show you how ready I am.

## CHILDHOOD

During childhood, our morals and ethics are shaped, demonstrated, and even practiced until approval is received from our parents. The shaping of our responses to *critical* events such as disapproval from friends or failure in a school subject and deciding courses of action for those and other trivial experiences are honed and refined until we reach a certain level of respect that both our parents and ourselves are comfortable with. *I can say with certainty that I thought I knew so much more than I actually did.* It is in our home that we are shown what love is, how to give and receive it. We have it demonstrated to us through positive and negative events, but nonetheless it is love.

Home is where we establish what we hold to be valuable and have worth…worth defending. For me, defending worth and value started with some kids poking fun at me with "mom" jokes. Those "jokes" have caused more than a couple of us to take the "green mile" trip to the principal's office, so I know you can relate. We see how Dad treats Mom and we hear how Mom talks to Dad. We hear the love in their voices or lack thereof. For me I saw how my grandfather used to put his hands on my grandmother's hips while she was looking into the refrigerator and whisper in her ear how much he loved her. I used to hear him greet her in the driveway after returning from work by saying "Hey there, beautiful!" (I can hear him say that like he is standing here) As a result, my wife hears those same words when she arrives home. I am a product of my environment. However, I am a product that I choose to be from that environment. It is my choice as an adult to either do as I was modeled after or not.

# PARENTS

Much of what we are, or what we try not to be, has been defined for us in our home. Some have had tough childhoods where there was a parent missing or there was strife between mother and father. Not every house has solid walls of protection from the world's influence. Parents are human too despite what our impressions are of them at the time. One of the hardest realizations that I had to come to grips with in becoming an adult was finding out that my parents weren't perfect. While they had all the right answers for me as a child, they themselves had made poor decisions in their own life. (Kaleb, Olivia and Ethan when you are old enough to read this book, you will have found out that, in fact, your father wasn't perfect by any stretch of the imagination… but I wanted perfection for you.) In that moment, my world became distorted. I asked myself "How can this be?" How can the perfect examples of adulthood that stood before me for eighteen years be imperfect? That answer didn't come quickly. Mostly that question and others were answered when I had kids of my own.

You've heard the expression "History repeats itself." Well, it could also apply in adulthood too. As we model the examples set for us by our parents, we believe them to be normal and everyday. Only until we walk out into the world and live in it do we find that "normal" is what we make of it. We can default to the prescribed thought that we are a product of our environment and thus relinquish ourselves to limitations that lie within. Or we can make conscious decisions to be different, to be better. It is our choice.

## OTHER INFLUENCES

Along with our parents, others also influence us like coaches, teachers, ministers, our close friends and their parents, etc. Together, they instill the foundation for purpose, meaning, and influence. I have had several coaches who have pushed me physically past points I thought I couldn't go. I have had teachers who encouraged me to take creativity to a higher level. I have had youth ministers who have helped me understand what being a trustworthy friend is. Yet among the influence, I still had EJ to deal with. His wants and desires would make themselves known and they were irresistible at times.

The shaping of purpose, meaning, and influence began molding for me what I mentioned earlier—value and worth. I began to lock in on what was valuable and what was of great worth. Of these, family and friends top the list. My family means the world to me, as I am sure yours does to you too. I would stop at nothing to defend them to include give up my life for them. If you have read *CounterViolence*, then you are familiar with the chapter in there called "A Hero's Death" where I explain what I am willing to die for in detail. I think it is a powerful chapter and for that reason I have placed it in its entirety in this book. If we are willing to give up our life for our family, I think it is important to explore the "Why would you" to be able to express how we truly feel about those we would die for and live a life (prior to that moment) that would be worth the cost of our precious life.

## MY HOME

For me, home held many facets. I grew up in Milton, Florida, a small town outside of Pensacola. Milton has a heavy military presence and Milton High School has a Navy flight trainer plane on its front lawn to show support for them. I mentioned earlier that my grandfather was an Army Air Corps B-24 pilot (the Army Air Corps was what preceded our US Air Force as we know it today), and, as you can imagine, had some military traits that stuck with him until the end. For example, my grandfather was a stickler for attention to detail, as well as "Say what you mean and mean what you say." When I would pack up to go to school the next day, he would come by my room and ask me if I had everything ready to go. Of course I did! That used to bug the mess out of me. Why did he feel the need to ask me this all the time? Well, it was because on more than one occasion he would get a call from me asking him to bring my baseball bag up the school so I would have it for practice. My oversight became his inconvenience. (My older son does the same thing now to me.) Along with his graciousness came a small lecture on attention to detail. (The same one my son gets from me.) This important task was later beaten into me by the big green machine (slang for the US Army) until it was a part of my very being. This was the beginning of learning preparedness. He used to tell me to physically touch all the items that I needed for the next day before retiring into the black hole called my room. Why touch it, you ask? Simple, because just looking at it wasn't enough for me. Sometimes I thought I saw it but somehow what I saw never made it to school. This would be valuable training that I would use everyday for the rest of my life and bestow to my children too. Still to this day I touch everything so I know beyond a shadow of a doubt I have it.

## LIFE

Home is where we practice for life. We experiment under the guidance of our parents who are there to pick us up after we fall. In some cases, they stand over us and tell us that they "told us so" before they pick us up (I'm sure you do the same thing with your kids, I do...I can't lie!).

I guess I could use the excuse that my dad left and my parents eventually divorced, I lived with my grandparents, I went to many different schools, and I was always the "new" guy everywhere I went to explain my outlandish actions as a child and thus use them as a way to gain pardon for my mistakes. I can honestly tell you that I wanted neither your pity nor your concern as I was going to make it on my own. I have an independent streak in me that has both helped me and caused me to miss out on some really great opportunities. All along, Momma and Papa were encouraging, mentoring, parenting, and correcting me... regardless of whether I wanted it or not. (Kaleb, Olivia, and Ethan, do you see where I get it from?)

## VALUE AND WORTH

It's in our home where we learn values and morals. *Value* is defined by *Merriam-Webster* as "relative worth, utility, or importance" and *moral* is defined as "concerning or relating to what is right and good in human behavior." For us as parents, we pass down our values and morals to our children not only in what we say but also in how we act. We demonstrate what has value to us by our actions and directions. My grandmother used to tell me to stop running in the house. I can see now at thirty-seven that it wasn't because I would break or destroy something, it was I could break or destroy someone—me! I could bust open my head, poke an eye out, or break a leg by running though our house and thus my kids get the same lecture from me on the same subject. I say all of this to say that living a life worth defending requires us to place worth before defending. Defining what is of worth is something we do consciously and subconsciously.

## FIRST THINGS FIRST

For me it starts with life. My parents believed life has a purpose and a meaning and that it is up to each individual to discover both and then to use them. I wholeheartedly agree and thus I live my life trying to bring purpose and meaning to my daily actions and influence. I don't believe things happen "just because." You are reading this book because there is a reason that you need to be reminded of these things. There is a reason I wrote this book, which is to put into words my feelings so you, my friends, and my children will read them and be reminded of what it is I value and will defend. I believe your life has a purpose and brings meaning to others, but it's what you make of it that determines whether or not at the end you lived it to its fullest.

## FAMILY

Second would be family. My family, as I am sure yours does too, means the world to me. It's family who supports you when the world says you can't, and it's family who stands by you in times of need. It's family that has the most sincere of congratulations when you succeed. So with that I say that it is family that you must defend. As a father I am the protector and provider, along with my wife, for our children. That is a responsibility that I hold in great esteem. I am so thankful for the opportunity to be a father!

But it is also family who can say things that hurt the most. It is also family, the ones who raised us and modeled for us what "right" was, who can betray our trust. This same family can turn against you and can influence you negatively. If you were not so fortunate as to have a supportive family, then maybe you have had to do things on your own and that can be difficult. My wife didn't have the things that I did growing up. She came from a broken home and moved around several times. She decided after high school that she needed structure and wanted to be pushed harder to succeed. Apparently she couldn't think of an easier place to gain those life skills so she enlisted into the United States Marine Corps.

After high school, she joined the Marines and traveled the globe, learning all she could about giving of herself for her unit, God, and country. She discovered things about her own character and developed strong positive values that would carry her through the rest of her life. She worked her way up the ranks through hard work and dedication and after twelve years left the Corps as a staff sergeant (Dad was an Army Infantry Officer and Mom was a Marine Corps Staff Sergeant…our children can't get a break!). She will tell you that life, family, country, and God are her priorities. It is these that she holds as valuable and worth defending, both with her actions and attitude, and even her life. As for my wife and I, we are on the same page for values and worth.

## YOUR LIFE

Think about your life for a moment. Was your childhood positive or negative? Did you have opportunities that you passed over because of one reason or another that you regret? I certainly do! Do you have purpose and meaning in your life now? Whatever your answers are, there is something you can do about it. Live life starting today by discerning worth and value then discover your purpose. Once you have your purpose, live it, don't exist around it. Life is precious and it is limited so start today making the best use of it. Find your influence and make it positive for others. Share with your children, spouse, friends, and others your experiences, both positive and negative, and how you over came adversity. We tend to keep negative things inside and disregard that others are going through the same thing. Trust me when I say they could use your encouragement. You are a powerful force in your own right and you can make a difference in someone else's life…including your own.

Be self-controlled and alert. Your enemy the devil prowls around like a roaring lion looking for someone to devour. Resist him, standing firm in the faith, because you know that your brothers throughout the world are undergoing the same kind of sufferings.

—1 Peter 5:8-9 (New International Version)

# 3

# THE JOURNEY

Definition:

**jour·ney** \ˈjər-nē\

*noun*

: an act of traveling from one place to another

WE ALL HAVE our own story of how we came to this very moment. Some stories are tragic and fraught with struggles; others are incredible stories of overcoming strife and persevering through heartaches. All have one thing in common, and that is you made it to here. This is the history of your journey and you have control over the future that lays in wait. The decisions we make and the actions we have toward others are what will determine your success or failure going forward. For all of us, we are in control of at least one thing and that is ourselves. We can control what we say, how we react, and what influence we have. This is a lesson that I, unfortunately, learned later in life.

After my grandfather passed away my senior year in high school, I went on to graduate and go off to college. I also enlisted in the Army National Guard. Being on my own and wearing a uniform should have opened my eyes to many of the things life would be demanding of me. Before I go on, I should mention that I am an "A" type personality and thus pretty headstrong. Well, I was pretty wrong in the perception that I had it all together. The world can be pretty cruel and unforgiving at times. I was on my way to figuring that out.

## "MOMMA"

My grandmother, who had been with my grandfather since age sixteen, was devastated after Papa's death. She withdrew from being the strong and independent woman that I knew growing up. She tried to stay active, but looking back, I can see that she was ready to go be with him. I was out and on my own when she went to live with her son (my uncle) in another state. I didn't keep in touch and our relationship drifted apart. This would come back to haunt me later in life. She was a wonderful woman with a doctorate in education and had been a teacher for as long as I can remember. She wrote many articles and was active in church teaching Sunday school. Thanks to her I have pretty good grammar skills and could carry on conversations with educated adults at a young age due to an expanded vocabulary. She wouldn't let me speak incorrectly and I detested how she was always correcting me.

## PRIORITIES

Somewhere along the way, she moved back to Memphis and we became pretty close again. When I did, she would want me to come over and stay with her. She would talk my ear off about Papa and their travels around the globe. As a young twenty-year-old, I had so many better things to be doing instead of hanging out with my grandmother. I would talk about my paramedic training and how bloody the stuff we were doing was. I loved to gross her out with that stuff! We never really fought. I guess it was because I respected her so much. So in that regard we had a great relationship. All of those times going over to see her and hearing her stories I can remember thinking "How can I tell here I have to go?" If I had only known that in a short two years' time she would be gone I would have done it all differently.

She was extremely lonely and starting to forget simple things on a regular basis. After some convincing by our family, she moved to Florida to live with another uncle of mine. It was during that time I got a call from my mother telling me she wasn't doing well and I should come down and see her. I flew to Orlando on the next available flight. When I arrived my uncles and aunts were all there and the mood was grim. It doesn't take a rocket surgeon to figure out what was coming. She had suffered from dementia in the last couple of years but it wasn't too bad so family took care of her. When I went in to see her one of my uncles put his arm around me and quietly told me that she wouldn't recognize me so I would be prepared.

I sat down next to her on her bed and she looked up at me and said, "Hey, baby, I'm so glad to see you."

"Hey, Momma" I said.

She grabbed my hand and smiled. We talked for about twenty minutes and she was alert unlike what my family had been seeing. I told her how much I loved her and how honored I was to be invited into her home and be raised by her. We cried together and hugged like tomorrow was already here. We shared so many meaningful things that I won't share with you because they are just between us. What she did tell me that I am so grateful to share with you is this: "Live your life with purpose, meaning, and influence." I count myself fortunate to have been able to express to her how much she meant to me and to hug her with sincere gratitude and love.

This strong woman that I had known all my life lay before me as a weak and struggling woman. After seeing her that day, I had to leave to get back to school, work, and the military. Two days after going back home I got the call. Momma had gone home to be with the Lord and Papa. I was sad for myself but happy for her.

# FRAGILE HEART

Death of a loved one is an experience we all have or will have in our life. You will die just as I surely will, but it is what we do while we are here that makes the difference. The ones we come in contact with, both good and bad, the ones we help or hurt, and the ones we love or push away, these interactions are how we leave our mark on Earth. All too often we look at what is done to us and what we do to others. I would ask that you flip that thought process and look at the "why."

Why did you say that?
Why did you act that way?
Why did you do that?

What is the commonality in all those questions? *You*! For it is in the "why" we find out what our true character is. Our heart is tender and sensitive and when someone or something breaks it, we retaliate against it/them.

Why is that? In most cases we are hurt, embarrassed, or even shamed. Our reaction is typically to "even the score" and hurt them as bad as they hurt us. It is performed with the false subconscious notion that we have time on our side to work it out later. If we have the same interaction but have it on our deathbed, would our reaction be the same? Or would there be understanding and forgiveness that we extend? I don't know for sure, but I have a pretty good guess that it wouldn't be so important. Let me pass on this bit of knowledge that I have learned throughout my career and that is this...

When the "why" becomes strong, the "what" becomes easy.

As a paramedic I saw more than my fare share of death, all different and all heartbreaking nonetheless. It is crucial to remember that tomorrow isn't promised for any of us. It is for that reason that extending the hand of reconciliation along your journey is so important. When we find ourselves staring death in the face, if we are lucky enough to get to do that, we will be filled with expressions of gratitude, forgiveness, and love for those close to us. We will want to tell them all how we really feel and how much they meant to us. I have seen it over and over again. Not only in my personal life but also as a paramedic. As a paramedic I have watched individuals die right in front of me and in some cases in my own arms. At that point, right before death, those who could talk have tried to express their love for their spouse, children, family, and friends. In most cases, those said words only fell on my ears. They never reached their intended audience.

## IMPACT

While I was a paramedic I responded to a call for "difficulty breathing." When we rolled up the fire truck was already there and the fire truck driver met us at the back of the ambulance while we were getting our gear and told me that it was a five-year-old girl in cardiac arrest. My partner and I grabbed our equipment and ran into the house to find CPR started on a beautiful blonde-haired, five-year-old girl lying in the living room floor an arm's length in front of the television. She was blue around the lips, her eyes had rolled back in her head, and she lay there lifeless. While I was putting an endotracheal tube down her throat to better get oxygen into her lungs, I happened to notice *Tom and Jerry* on the TV.

Her parents were standing in the kitchen, which over-looked the living room where we were working, crying and hugging. My partner put the EKG cables on her chest while I started administering our protocol drugs through an IV. The EKG showed a ventricular fibrilla-tion rhythm and by our standards I administered shocks from the defibrillator in an attempt to correct it to a normal life-sustaining rhythm. We moved her to the ambulance and kept giving her shocks from the defibrill-lator and administering every drug we could. We were pushing oxygen into her lungs and performing CPR in conjunction but nothing was working.

Time is critical and we have to manage it ruthlessly in order to have the greatest chance at saving her. From our location, we were too far from the children's hospi-tal, which is where our local protocol says we have to go, so I called in the hospital wing. It was during the transport to the impromptu landing zone at the local Walmart that her heart gave out and stopped fighting. The EKG went into a flat line and, just like in the movies you might have seen; there was a long consistent eerie tone erupting from the machine. Everyone in the back of my ambulance knew what that meant.

The hospital wing is the air ambulance for the Memphis regional area. We drove over to the Walmart parking lot where the hospital wing sat down. As the flight nurse climbed in, I gave her all the stats and protocols administered up to that point. (These are some of the best RNs in the business.) The ambulance was filled with emergency personnel working together to save this innocent girl's life. Firemen were doing compressions and getting supplies; my partner was breathing for her using a bag valve mask and oxygen while I was administering drugs and checking her cardiac status consistently.

She checked my data and evaluated my patient. I felt her hand go on my shoulder as I took over performing CPR. I looked up and asked her if she was ready to move to the helicopter. She compassionately looked at me and said, "She's gone...there's nothing more we can do. You have been at his for forty-five minutes with no response." She turned to the fire department lieutenant (LT) on scene and said, "I'm calling it...time of death is—"

I screamed at her "No! You can get her there but you have to go now!" I will never forget her next words to me.

"EJ, you have done all you could do, we are not going to be able to bring her back. She's gone!"

My LT came around to the side door of my ambulance. "Come on, brother, you have to let her go!" he said.

I stopped CPR and looked at the monitor, looked at the flight nurse, and dropped my head in utter exhaustion. I took a sheet out and draped it over her body. As everyone was exiting the ambulance, I sat and stared at the sheet I had just laid. I said a prayer over her and told her I was sorry that there wasn't anything else I could do.

Outside waiting on me were my brother firemen and partner and together we cried. Like in every career you have highs and lows and through it all you have to get back up and keep moving. After that call we cleaned up and restocked back at the fire station and got ready for the next call.

I later found out that this same little girl went to my church and my uncle was her pastor. I asked him if it would be inappropriate to go to her funeral to pay my respects. I stood in the back for a little while and listened as her mom told cute stories of her and how blessed they were to have her for the short time they did. I had to leave...I couldn't take it anymore. I felt like a failure. I played the "What if" game for months. What if we had gotten there sooner? What if I had done this or that better? What if I had pumped harder on her chest? These questions would never get answered. What took me by surprise was the finality of death. At a young age I had had a front row seat to what is in store for all of us and more importantly...that it is final.

I think about how much impact that little girl had on her parents, teachers, friends, and family, and how much it continues to mean to them. Look at the impact it had on me. So much so that I put it in this book. Now you are reading about it. We never know how far our impact reaches. We all share that same impact in some way or another with our own life. I challenge you not to wait to make that impact. Rather, start today, by bringing purpose, meaning, and influence to everyone you encounter. In some small way, you can bring something positive to their life and in return do the same for yourself.

# ENCOURAGEMENT

Your journey is not over yet. You still have things to do while you are here and you should be about doing it until your time is up. I hope that when my time is called and I must leave you all that I can honestly say I've done all that I could do, said everything that I've wanted to say, and demonstrated through my actions love and compassion for those I have been with. It is a tough task to accomplish and will continue to evoke humility and compassion on my part, but I do believe in making this a better place than when I found it by seeing the good in my everyday life and telling others about it. Could it be that someone will be encouraged to overcome heartbreak or carry on through a difficult time by my words or actions? I may never know but I have to try.

If you decide to carry the same cross through your life you may never know either, but you will carry a sense of joy you have never experienced before I promise you that. You may not always know what to say or what to do. I understand as I am still going through life too! I can tell you that when you focus on "why" you do and say the things you do, the "what" to do and say will come easy.

Extend the hand of reconciliation to those who have hurt you, forgive them even if they do not accept your apology. Love like there is no tomorrow and express how much you love those around you. A great starting place is to make peace with yourself, your family, and with God.

> Forgiveness can be a few words away, but you have to speak it to find out.

Don't wait for a better time or to think of a better way. Don't wait for them to right their wrong. Your journey is what you make of it and is not dependent on someone else. You can make the rest of your journey meaningful and full of purpose, but it's up to you.

# 4

# CHAINS THAT BIND

Definition:

**chain** \ˈchān\

*noun, often an attribute*

: a series of usually metal links or rings that are connected to each other in a line and used for supporting heavy things, for holding things together, for decoration, etc.
: a chain that is attached to the arms or legs of a prisoner
: a series or group of things or people that are connected to each other in some way

THERE ARE SO many things in life that cause us to look back and say, "I wish I had done that differently." I know this firsthand. I have looked back many times on events and relationships that I was a part of and knew that I hadn't made something positive out of it. My selfishness and my ego have kept me from experiencing a lot that life had to offer during those times. Sounds an awful lot like regret, huh? I believe that regret can be as much, if not more, of a hindrance in going forward than the events of the past could ever be. Regret is like a fifty-pound weight that rides low on your back, persistent in its quest to bring you down. It is relentless and painful. Others may not be able to see it but inside it screams at us that we have failed in some way or another. These regrets make it difficult to stand strong during trials and tribulations. We can't find the right words to say. We can't find something to hold on to in order to give us stability in times of need.

These little pinpricks of regret all compile on our self-confidence and slowly chip away at our perception of accomplishing something great. I didn't realize how much it chipped away at mine until I went into the Army. During training, the Army likes to consistently take you outside of your comfort zone to show you that either you don't need to be here, or, conversely, that you can actually succeed doing something you thought you couldn't do. I spent almost ten years as an enlisted soldier learning to complete tasks to perfection and to put the mission and my unit over the wants of myself. I didn't finish college right away because I was chasing wants and desires that were frivolous. I finally finished my bachelor's degree in business management at twenty-six. I finally found determination to finish and did so easily thanks to some financial support from the Army. My platoon leader introduced a program called Officer Candidate School (OCS) and managed to somehow convince me that I would make a good military officer. I enrolled into OCS and graduated in the top of my class in academics and physical fitness.

## BUTTER BAR

After OCS, I was commissioned as a second lieutenant and headed off to Ft. Benning, Georgia, for the four-month Infantry Officer Basic School (IOBC). During IOBC, we had many graded leadership tasks and physical fitness requirements that were difficult for most. Now, let me just say that there are some guys blessed from birth with great physical stamina and book smarts and you have them in every class. I am not one of those individuals. I have to work very hard at both. Leadership, on the other hand, is something that has to be modeled, practiced, and refined. Just ask any platoon sergeant what one of his first statements to a new lieutenant is and they will tell you it goes something like this: "Hello, sir! Welcome to your new platoon. You will go far in this unit if you will learn to keep your mouth closed, watch, learn and speak only when it's appropriate. When you do speak, speak clearly and in a tone which displays confidence and the men will follow. If they don't I'll take care of it. If you have any good questions, ask me and I will help you. Otherwise, stand over there and let us do our job!" I'm paraphrasing, of course, but you get the point. Confidence is key! Confidence comes from repeated overcoming of adversity.

## ONE STEP AT A TIME

In IOBC, we had to do a night land navigation course (map reading and navigating from one point to another while traversing rugged terrain by yourself) that has so many points to find with just your compass that you had to start at eight that night (2000) and finished somewhere around four in the morning (0400). It was during this course that my doubts and regrets compiled on me and set me up for a life-changing event.

I had been walking around the woods of Ft. Benning for hours, finding points and heading out toward the next one. I was tired and hungry and in the Army that is a sure sign you will soon start feeling sorry for yourself. I was lacking confidence in completing this course before the sun comes up. That would mean by Army standards I was a "No Go" (i.e., failure). I would have one more chance to do it again before being recycled to the next class.

I was deep in the woods. The foliage was thick enough to block the moonlight from shining on my compass, which I needed to keep my direction. I ended up stumbling down a deer trail into a dry creek bed about twelve feet below where I was once walking. Falling twelve feet in the dark is not fun, trust me on that one. I tried several times to climb out on the other side but the bank was too steep. I had to move about thirty-five yards off my direction of travel to find a way up.

I found some saplings growing on the bank and, using them, I pulled myself up. Well, I got up on the other side, all right…right into a sticker bush thicket. I think the infantry school plants those things on purpose…but I digress. They were so thick that I was crawling on my hands and knees one step at a time and going nowhere fast. With the little moonlight that was peeking through, I saw the little green eyes of the spiders looking back at me and they were all round. Not that I'm scared of spiders, but it is creepy nonetheless. I got hung up with those sticker bushes catching my clothing, bootlaces, and even my face. I was bleeding, tired, hungry, and frustrated. It is interesting what your inner monologue comes up with when you feel trapped and have no direction. At one point I started thinking of a time in baseball where I had walked the winning run, in college where I had not studied as hard as I should have and made a less than desirable grade, and relationships where it was purely my fault when it fell apart. I thought about how I would tell my wife why I would be getting recycled from this course. All of these thoughts centered on my self-pity and were only enhanced by my physical fatigue. Quitting has never been easier to do than in times like these. I seriously considered using that strobe light the TAC Officers (OCS instructors are called TAC Officers. TAC stands for Teach, Assess, and Counsel) had given us to use if we had a medical emergency or were really lost. I could turn it on and eventually a helicopter using night vision would find me and direct the rescue party to my location for extraction. So many things were going through my head because I had lost confidence in myself.

Surely most of the guys had finished by now and were doing the rucksack flop (laying on your back resting) in the training area waiting on me to finish. I had bled enough. I was tired and I was constrained in my movements. I rolled over on my back inside of that sticker bush thicket and put my hands over my face. I was really feeling sorry for myself on a stupid land navigation course. Ridiculous, I know! We never know when these feelings will culminate and shut you down and for me it was right here. Thankfully no one was around to see me. After about five minutes, which seemed like two hours, I said to myself, "Okay, enough with that stuff, it's time to pick it up and keep moving!" I started focusing on each step as its own victory. I put out of my mind the totality of the situation and concentrated on just what I could control, which was me. One step at a time, one cut at a time, is what I saw as one victory at a time. I slowly made my way out of it. On what would be my last step (I'm still crawling at this point), I looked up and saw a huge clearing with lights about three hundred yards away. I could hear voices talking and laughing. I checked my map, identified certain terrain features, and found my position. In between where I was and where the lights were was my last point. There standing in the middle of this clearing was my last point to record. I headed toward the voices. I thought to myself, *The lights had to be the end.* I got up on both feet and moved out with a purpose. As I came into the lights I saw a couple of guys doing the rucksack flop (lying on their backs against their rucksacks) and one student with his ankle wrapped in white gauze.

My TAC officer came over to me and said, "Owens, is that you?"

"Yes, sir!" I replied tiredly.

He asked for my point sheet and proceeded to verify that I had reached all my points. "Owens, you're a Go!" I heard. I had finished ahead of most of the students. He asked me, "Did you come through the thicket?"

A questionable "Yes, sir" came out of my mouth.

"Why did you choose that route? You could have circled the ridge and walked in," he replied.

I was too tired to give a "high speed" answer and so the truth ensued. "I didn't choose the thicket, sir, it chose me." In this simple time of despair, I was ready to stop and give in to my self-pity, all because I let my previous failures lead me to believe that I couldn't do it. All along the end was in a clearing three hundred yards away.

## MY DECISION

In life our own perception of past failure can lead to actual future failure if we give in to it. There was some difficulty, but it wasn't impossible by any stretch of the imagination and I made it out to be in my mind. When I got up on my feet is when I made a mental and physical decision not to let that control me. It was simply a decision. I decided that I would accept those previous failures but from this point on I would try to do right by myself and others. I've never told this story before because it can be embarrassing as it involves self-doubt and the air of quitting—both unacceptable by Army Officer standards—during a simple undertaking. By the course standards, I was a success, but what I took away from it was so much more. I control my drive and my ultimate destiny. I would use those lessons throughout the rest of my time in the Army and in other situations life would have in store for me later on down the road. I went on to graduate IOBC and became a United States Army Infantry Officer.

## CHANCES

Every one of us is unique in our own right. We all have failures that plague us at some point then leave and others that stay with us for quite awhile. They will eventually weigh you down so much that you can't jump on that opportunity of a lifetime staring you in the face. Don't spend your time looking back. I encourage you to let it all out and deal with it for what it is. Don't hold in your anger. Don't hold in your sadness. Change the things you can and accept that which you cannot. In life I have taken chances, as I'm sure you have as well. Because of those chances we have been praised, accepted, despised, and rejected. It takes guts to take chances because the fear of failure is real and harsh. The Army was fantastic at proving to me that "true character is judged not in how one acts when things are going their way but when things are against them."

You know the things in your past that bother you. Bad decisions in close relationships, inappropriate attitudes in the work place, putting your immediate wants over the good of others, and many more. They happened. Don't run from the truth because you can't get away. Give them their due then put them in the appropriate place and leave them alone. This is important in getting your life ready to defend it. Make peace with yourself on these things and make peace with your close friends and family. Regret has no place in the defense of your life.

It will cause you to hesitate during a small window of opportunity. It will weigh you down and keep you from being bold in the face of death.

Live in the moment of your small victories and count yourself as blessed. When you attend your son's little league game, when you sit beside your daughter during her first driving lesson, when you dance with your spouse for no reason in the kitchen, recognize these as positive memories being made that will stay with those special people in your life long after you are gone. Don't let the chains of the past bind you from experiencing these times in all of their glory. In the end it is how you live your life that will determine your legacy. Wake up to the sunlight and start tomorrow off by releasing those chains and focusing on the good that you bring to others. You control your thoughts and emotions, you control regret and you can forgive yourself. To start living a life worth defending, you must first realize that you have been broken at times, recognize the journey that has brought you to this point, and release the chains that bind you from experiencing life to its fullest.

You may encounter many defeats, but you must not be defeated. In fact, it may be necessary to encounter the defeats, so you can know who you are, what you can rise from, how you can still come out of it.

—Maya Angelou

# 5

# INNER BEAST

THERE LIVES WITHIN all of us an inner beast. This is the beast of anger and rage. He can be demanding of our time, thoughts, and actions if not controlled. From the psychobiological point of view, it probably had its survival utility in early times, but it seems to have lost a lot of it in modern societies. Actually, in most cases, it is counterproductive, even dangerous.

## ANGER

Anger is a feeling that we all encounter from time to time, and frequently we experience it as a response to frustration, hurt, disappointment, and threats (real or imagined). Anger in healthy persons is diminished through action. It is an aversive, unpleasant emotion. It is intended to generate action in order to eradicate this uncomfortable sensation. Anger is induced by numerous factors. It is almost a universal reaction. Any threat to one's welfare (physical, emotional, social, financial, or mental) is met with anger. But so are threats to one's affiliates, nearest, dearest, nation, favorite football club, pet, and so on. The territory of anger is enlarged to include not only the person, but all of his real and perceived environment, human and nonhuman. Anger is the reaction to injustice (perceived or real), to disagreements, to inconvenience. But the two main sources of anger are malice threats and innocent injustice.

## RAGE

Rage is the accumulation of unexpressed anger and perceived disrespectful transactions that after multiple "stuffings of ones emotions" finally flow to the surface. When we become enraged, usually there is the belief that someone is deliberately attempting to incite us to become angry. Within this ego-bruised state, we are convinced that trying to be reasonable will prove to be ineffective and therefore we will need to "even the score" or methodically disarm the offending party.

## CONTROL

In a self-defense situation, it is common that the audacity alone that the attacker/s have to assault you causes anger to turn to rage in seconds. As anger transforms into rage, it causes you to loose the mental perception to devise a survival plan and…stick to it. In a gunfight, skill and ability take a backseat to the mental alertness needed to coordinate decisive actions. A gunfight is as much a mental chess match as it is an aggressive physical confrontation. When we lose control of our mental state we lose control of our ability to make conscious and calculated counterviolence decisions.

On the range you are learning to control a weapon and its nuances, but along the way you must learn how to control your emotions and keep it together long enough to win all three battles of the fight—Physical, Emotional, and Legal. If you let the beast out and he's not on a leash, he will surely cause you great harm, both in the short term and the long. Our emotions are like a powerful muscle that must be worked out and trained. In order to control the beast, you have to let him out once in a while and take him for a walk. However, just like an attack dog, you must keep a tight leash on him or he will hurt someone or you.

During my live training courses, I often take students outside their comfort zones to see how they react. This catches them by surprise and I often see some real emotions. There is no way for them to prepare for it…it just happens and therefore the emotional reactions are raw and pure. From there, because we are in a controlled environment, we can review them together and discuss a better way to control them so that the outcome is as favorable as the situation will allow. Unless we train ourselves to handle the extreme emotional stress we will encounter we are taking a great risk at poor performance.

If you have kids like I do, you have seen them on Christmas morning when they are opening presents and they are as joyful as the will ever be all year. Conversely, when you punish them for a wrong by taking away something they really enjoy playing with, they have a meltdown. You see crying, screaming, and maybe some sort of physical acting out. I hate to say it but that could be you in a fight for your life if you haven't trained your emotions to handle things "not going your way." People are as different as snowflakes so everyone will react differently in one way or anther but we can stereotype to a degree. You have the ones who act out and ones who shut down. The ones who act out can be trained to control those emotions and focus them to achieve positive results. It might take great concerted efforts but nonetheless can be achieved. The ones who shut down, on the other hand, have a tougher hill to climb in my opinion.

## SHUTTING DOWN

Shutting down is your body saying, "I can't take all this stress anymore." It's a numb feeling. People get it when they are so overwhelmed that they just can't deal with things anymore. Your emotions are there to guide you and keep you on the right track and when you suppress them you are left in an emotional purgatory. I will tell you that your "gut feeling" is an emotional response manifesting itself through a physical manner. Your emotions are guiding you in order to protect you from something. Don't deny your feelings…just keep them under control.

When you feel anger, try to move through the events that brought you there. Understanding is important to us as humans. It has helped us discover miracles of modern medicine, architectural design feats, and even allowed us to walk on the moon. Our quest to understand our environment is only second to our desire to understand ourselves. During firearms training, we are discovering our environment and how to use it to gain advantage (i.e., cover, concealment, makeshift weapons, improvised medical solutions, etc.), but we also need to discover what our emotions are going to be like during the encounter in order to use them to gain advantage.

Through our anger or rage, we might decide our only alternative is to run right at the guy holding the gun when cover was to the left of us allowing us to change positions and continue devising a better plan of attack or defense. Your attacker has a plan (however loose it is) and he is trying to stick to it. That plan involves you doing what he wants you to do. When we can control our fear, anger, and rage, we maintain control of our mental state and allow us precious time to devise a plan of counterviolence.

# RECOGNITION

The next time you are in an environment where you are failing (game, work, class of instruction, etc.), try to recognize your frustration level and whether or not you just want to give up, quit, or even walk away and forget about attempting it ever again. If you experience these then you are human and there is nothing to be ashamed of...I still feel them too! However, it is what you do with those feelings that determine your overall success or failure. My grandfather used to ask me this question when I was overwhelmed: "EJ, how do you eat an elephant?" to which I would respond, "I don't know," before I figured it out on my own. "One bite at a time!" he replied. Deal with your emotions one at a time and soon you will be able to control them to aid you in achieving your goal.

1. Accept it: "I am angry."

   To deny or suppress anger is counterproductive and dangerous. Allow yourself to experience and express it respectfully. Irrational expression of anger is a choice.

2. Seek to understand it: What is this about?

   Is it on the job, at home, everywhere? Is this degree of anger really appropriate to communicate my concern?

3. Devise an action plan: Don't ignore it do something.

   Visualize one or more acceptable solutions. Ask yourself:

   • Do I really want to stay angry or move on?

   • Do I want others to remember me as out of control and disrespectful?

Remember:
> Repressed anger (the precursor to rage) lives on as resentment and blocks the ability to engage in constructive problem solving.

## A Gunfight Is Problem Solving at Its Finest!

We all experience fear, dread, sorrow, sadness, and more, but when we allow those to control our actions, we tend not to succeed and in some cases miss out on greatness that was just around the corner. Control the beast!

When anger rises, think of the consequences.

—Confucius

# 6

# WORTH IT ALL

As a father, I try my best to rear my kids to be self-respecting, compassionate leaders. If you are a parent then you understand that even with our best efforts we often fall short. My children are all "A"-type personalities and thus tend to have their own understanding of how they should solve their problems. When I get asked to interject my opinion, you can bet that the problem is pretty far down the track. As with any parent, we want to help them be successful in their endeavors. What I have found, through being a military officer, business owner, and parent, is that your leadership is more in your example than in your words. In my family we have a saying, "Your actions are speaking so loud I can't hear what you're saying." That is to say that the tone of your voice and the roll of your eyes, coupled with your hands on your hips, are saying "I don't want to and I'll only do it if you are making me," while your mouth is saying, "Fine, I'll do it, Dad." Now, let me say this, I'm not a super Dad at all! I make mistakes all the time. However, my actions directly reflect my beliefs and priorities. Think about it.

"Wherever your priorities go...actions follows."

Kids see what you do. They study you. You are their role models for social interactions, morals, marriage, the list goes on. As they grow up you find yourself listening to your kids say the same quirky sayings you say, yet they sound so different coming from your kids and not you. Often I have asked my wife, "Do I sound like that?" As with sayings, comes the mimicking of actions too.

## A WAY OF LIFE

I have been carrying concealed for as long as my kids can remember. It is so ingrained, as it is a priority so my actions follow, in my kids' heads that Dad always has a gun on that they don't think twice about it. It's like it's a body part that naturally is a part of me. My daughter is a big hugger and on more than one occasion she has remarked, "Dad, why don't you have your gun on?" to which I will tell her that I just got out of the shower and am heading to bed. The important thing is that she has come to expect it. My wife and I talk to them about why we carry and what our guns are really for. As I said earlier though, my actions are speaking so loudly that she can't hear what I am saying. It's what we do because of who we are. There is no bravado or power trip associated with it. We don't make it out to be anymore than it really is. We carry concealed to give us an opportunity to continue living and taking care of our family should someone decide that they wanted to take that away from us.

Too often the mindset and discussions in the gun community are centered on the act of defending yourself from a band of rogue animals hell bent on removing you from the planet. We discuss in infinite detail skills, tactics, gear, training regimens, etc. What I feel is important is the lifestyle *prior* to the self-defense act and the understanding of why we did what we did *after* the act. Your life, as an example of your beliefs and principals, will tell people what they need to know but it has to be lived first. Your life is your legacy. Should you not make it out of the gunfight, I believe you would want to know that you did, said, and expressed everything you ever wanted to those who you want to say it to. Even more so should you find yourself sitting in a jail cell alone with just your thoughts…you are at peace. In most self-defense classes, they mainly focus on the skill development for the fight—stance, grip, sight alignment, trigger control, follow-through, scan, assess, and the list just keeps on going. We neglect to delve into the before and the after. This is where we need to help out each other and ourselves.

Everyday carry is a lifestyle choice, not an act we perform when we are going to the "bad parts of town." It should be a part of you that is as routine as putting your wallet in your back pocket. So much so that your daughter hugs you and asks why you don't have it on. A lifestyle choice that in turn helps to define the ultimate question of gunfight survivors, "Was it worth it all?" I have been asked about carrying in places that post a sign saying not to. I have been asked about carrying wearing a suit versus shorts and flip-flops. My answer is always the same…I carry! Certainly I run the risk of being found out and getting into potentially serious trouble, but the benefits outweigh the risks in my mind. Should I have to deal with a life-threatening situation I want everything I can bring to aid in staying alive. Now, I don't advocate doing anything illegal. You need to follow all local, state, and federal rules regarding concealed carry. However, I will put it to you like this…I would much rather continue to see my children and help shape their lives for the better even if it is from behind a bulletproof window talking on a telephone. But that is a personal decision and not one that I force you to adopt or accept.

I have to weigh the question within myself. Was it worth it all? Are my kids still alive? Is my life worth it? The answers to those and others are still yet to be determined until the conflict arises. My kids and wife know that this is a lifestyle choice and it comes with risk. A risk could be that I might inadvertently expose my weapon and get caught. One risk is that I might have to shoot someone who is trying to kill others or myself in a "gun-free zone." In that case, I just have to take my chances with our legal system and hope for the best. It is much better than standing at my nine-year-old daughter's casket saying, "If I'd only carried." This, again, is a personal decision. When I am sitting in that jail cell awaiting bond out or trial I have to deal with the man in the mirror and he is the hardest to please. I have to know that what I did was right from a personal moral decision so that I can be at peace regardless of the legal decision of my fate. I have to know that I have said how I feel to the ones I love, that I have lived the life I needed to in order to be the best possible example to my children, and I have lived according to my spiritual beliefs. I have lived and not merely existed.

## YOUR TIME

Keep in mind what I said earlier, you may not survive, and much like dying, being in a jail cell for the rest of your life is pretty much the same to the ones who love you. If you are too busy to go to the game or the play your kids are in, you will live with that regret for the rest of your life. If you are spending your time chasing the finer things in life and it takes away from your home time, you will regret that too. Remember, your time equals relationships, memories, and influence, all of which you give up chasing material things. As for me, I would rather live in a shack built upon a rock over a castle on the sand. If you are that person that is working too much to spend quality time with your family, I would ask you this: Is chasing the American dream giving you worth? You are running out of time and I pray you start using it wisely.

## WHAT IF?

In your training, you need to visualize this after your drill is over. You need to practice your skills certainly but also you need to stretch your emotional muscles. Envision what happens if you fail. How the lives of your loved ones are forever changed. I do this and it drives me to reject mediocrity in my training. It demands perfection. It also helps me to understand what I will go through should the law not agree with my actions. It prepares me to deal with the emotional distress I might experience sitting in jail. I understand that this is not the norm in the gun community. I get it! However, it doesn't make it any less of a reality to those who have been there.

In my military career, I was taught to train for the unexpected as well as the expected. We play the "What if" game in every scenario we perform. This aids in decision making under stress. Using parallel experiences, we use deductive reasoning to help drill down on the possible solution by eliminating the known and focusing on the unknowns. We draw from similar life experiences to help us make educated decisions in areas we are having difficulty deciding the best course of action.

> As a child, you tried to control events in your life to give you experiences. As an adult, you use your experiences to control events.

If we experience these emotions in a controlled environment and under experienced supervision, then we can correct our mistakes and hone our craft in a superior way. Our task as a concealed carrier is to be more prepared, better trained, and emotionally superior than our enemy, thus giving us a higher chance of victory. We commit everything we are in the moment because we have taken care of everything prior to and we have already calculated the cost. We are prepared to pay it... even with our life! Are you at that point in your life? If so, congratulations! If not, there are three things you can do that will help you.

- Make peace with yourself.
- Make peace with your family.
- Make peace with God.

This is the starting point. Next, you need to prepare yourself for the fight by getting into shape. Start eating right. Get your sleep regularly. Train like your life depends on it. Hopefully, if it is ever asked of you "Was it worth it all?" you will be at peace with your answer.

# 7

# GUARDING THE DOOR

**THERE MIGHT COME** a time when all your training, experience, courage, and determination will be called into one act of self-defense. It will happen fast. It will be upon you without advance warning. Your next actions will determine your continued existence here on planet Earth. Your ability to move off the threat vector, utilize the given space, calculate the relative time till impact, and judge the force being applied to counteract the aggression will be in a split second. I cannot emphasize enough how you not "rise to the occasion" but rather you will default to the highest level you have mastered. Your threat recognition skills will aid you in the next few steps you must enact to survive. Too often we as protectors lull ourselves into the false sense of security that we can act with a victorious outcome in a true self-defense situation because we can successfully hit paper at seven yards at a static range with a box of fifty rounds bought at our local gun range. That is not gunfighting!

In order to truly guard the door, you must push past your level of comfort in training and hit failure points. When you hit those failure points is the time when true growth takes place. Will you tighten down your focus and work to push past it or will you go back down to a level where you are successful and stay there because it is comfortable? Be honest with yourself here. I can't tell you what your fight is going to look like. It might be as simple as one bad guy at seven yards like your static range experience, but it might be four bad guys at a traffic light carjacking you and shooting your daughter in the backseat. Bad guys are getting bolder and taking more risks and therefore you have to up your training game. As the protector of your own life and the lives of your family, you have to take the initiative to push yourself to be better and quicker and more accurate under stress. Here is where having a group of training partners helps to push your comfort limits and hold you accountable. I have a group of great people that I train with and I highly recommend you do too.

## WARRIOR

I see you as a warrior. Warriors train and train hard. Throughout my military career, I have failed more times than my successes. I can be honest with you here. The failures are a result of pushing myself to be faster, more accurate, and ultimately more lethal in a self-defense situation. That comes through failure! If you look at how our society is evolving, you are a dying breed. Our social brother and sisters are waiting for a white knight with blue lights and badges to save them from evil. As I am sure you are aware, the white knights are not coming in the moment. It's up to you to guard the door!

## THE BIG "3"

There are three tiers to guarding your door that we need to explore. First, the situational awareness that comes from watching your local news is paramount. You have to understand what types of criminals are lurking and what your local police and sheriff's department are doing to combat them. This lays the groundwork for the type of defense you need to establish as a baseline. Criminals are not original in their thought and therefore follow others and their successes. Police stats show that there are crime "waves" that come and go. Watching your local news gives you a heads up on what they are trying to do to the sheeple in your neighborhood and community.

Secondly, you need to evaluate your own family security requirements. How many people are you responsible for? How many of them are adults who are capable of being responsible for their own protection? Do you have children who need your security? What about adults who refuse to protect themselves? Now, if you just gave a big huff about that last question, I truly understand. I have immediate family members who live in fantasyland too! Nonetheless, as a protector, as a sheepdog, I will defend them if I am available and capable. Let's stop for a second so I can bring up a point or two about understanding your own family security requirements. I have small children and if the fight were to come to me while I am caring for them then I might have to engage the threat one-handed while securing my children. I think about these situations when I am training. With that in mind, I work a lot on shooting one-handed. Think about how many times you have been driving only to have to stop suddenly and you reach your hand across the passenger seat to brace your passenger. You will do the same thing in defense of your child or wife if presented with a deadly encounter. You will want to grab and pull close to you that which you will protect. Train like that!

Third is your own physical ability. If you are out of shape, overweight, or even unobservant, then you are giving an advantage to your attacker that you don't have to. Take it upon your self, as a warrior should, to improve in these areas. Not only will you increase your chances in surviving but you might actually live longer and enjoy life a little more in the process. Too many times I see students come out to my live shooting classes and they haven't done anything to prepare for the "fight." The Modern Warrior Experience class that we hold every so often starts off with fighting and ends with fighting even more. The point of it is to be prepared to give all that you have to live another day. There is this misconception that the fight will involve taking two steps to the left, draw from open carry position, and successfully engage a static, nonshooting target with two shots and then be rushed off to a parade in your honor. That is simply not the case. Take charge of your lifestyle and your physical prowess.

## BEYOND

If you are at a level of proficiency that allows you to be successful, then it's time to push beyond it and meet failure face to face. I welcome failure in my classes and find it refreshing when the student wants to "do the drill again" in order to beat it. I like a strong desire to push limits. Within the spectrum of pushing limits, there lies pushing the limits of your family to become more observant, more aware, and more alert. They are not going to magically develop those capabilities overnight. You have to educate them.

Point things out and make them aware of what to look for. Demonstrate how they should act. Develop action plans and rehearse them. Dry run them in your home. Talk about them and start the conversation. Your involvement and enthusiasm will drive their curiosity, and in the long run make them better suited to recognize a bad situation when it starts to develop. The best thing that you can do for others is to pass along your knowledge. If after that you can add to their skill and proficiency then even better. As said many times in the cartoon *GI Joe*, "Knowledge is half the battle." There is truth to that.

There are things that you may only need to know one time in your life but could save your life because you had that knowledge. You carry with you knowledge that needs to be pasted around. With knowledge comes power. Share what you know so that we continue to build a nation of warriors. Guarding the door should be a shared responsibility, but it starts with you. You are the guardian, and in order to increase your survival, you need more eyes watching and more hands acting alongside you. We need more of you in our world!

# 8

# A HERO'S DEATH

DEATH TEACHES US so much about life and about ourselves, even though it can be very difficult to compre-
hend and experience. As a culture we don't really talk
about death, deal with it, or face it in an authentic way.
Death often seems too scary, mysterious, personal,
loaded, heavy, emotional, tragic, and more.

The thought of death can be detrimental to us in a
gunfight. It can cause us to hold in a position of cover
and panic losing the advantage of movement, allowing the attackers actions to control your OODA Loop
resulting in your demise. So because of the fear of death
we die without a well-fought fight. Personally I will not,
while there is still a breath left in me, allow these animals to ruthlessly murder my family or me while I stand
by out of fear for my own safety. I will commit, in the
moment, everything that I am to ending the threat to
my family and myself. This commitment is only realized
by controlling fear.

There is a fine line that separates *fear* from *courage*.
Courage is action is spite of fear. You truly do not know

how you will react in a deadly encounter because we can't replicate the amount of physiological and emotional duress that you will be under in a training environment. However, you can learn to control any emotional deviation from your training that you might experience with a clear and decisive mindset. A mindset of determination and courage will aid you greatly through "events" but the real key to survival is to live, live fully with no regrets. Commit now, this minute, before you continue to read this book that you will live your life to its fullest.

I have seen death in many of its forms. I have seen innocence die and those whom probably deserved to die slow and painfully, i.e. rapist and child molester ("deserved" is based on my own moral and ethical code). While we have all known someone who has died, most of us separate ourselves from that experience. We just do not like to think about it. After all, it is a long way off, right? So we walk around on autopilot, caught up in the business—the busyness—of life. However, when we finally believe that we are going to die, we see things much differently. I have held those dying in my arms and watched their soul leave their body both innocent and the deserved. I can tell you this, most of them at the point they recognized that it was their time instantly were filled with regret.

Regret is a negative cognitive/emotional state that involves blaming ourselves for a bad outcome, feeling a sense of loss or sorrow at what might have been or wishing we could undo a previous choice that we made. Over short time periods, people are more likely to regret actions taken and mistakes made, whereas over long time periods, they are more likely to regret actions not taken, such as missed opportunities for love or working too hard and not spending enough time with family.

Along with their regret is a longing for forgiveness and to forgive. People hurt us intentionally and unintentionally. While we need to correct people who have views that can be divisive and ill informed, it does not mean we need to wipe them out of consciousness. Relationships don't last long if we kill off those who have hurt us. Since relationships are what make life meaningful, we benefit most when we tolerate the idea that people we love are capable of both good and bad.

**Accept what you are able to do and not able to do.**
**Accept the past without denying it or discarding it.**
**Learn to forgive yourself and to forgive others.**
**Do not assume that it is too late to get involved.**

What if we embraced death our own and of those around us in a real, vulnerable and genuine way? What if we lived life more aware of the fact that everyone around us, including ourselves, has a limited amount of time here on earth? Embracing death consciously alters our experience of ourselves, others and life in a fundamental and transformational way. It allows us to remember what truly matters and to put things in a healthy and empowering perspective. Doing this is much better for us than spending, perhaps wasting our time worrying, complaining, and surviving the circumstances, situations, and dramas of our lives, isn't it?

The fruit of belief is action. And the benefit of learning how to die physically is to learn how to live spiritually. If faith is part of your life, express it in ways that seem appropriate to you. You may find comfort and hope in reading spiritual texts, attending religious services or praying. Allow yourself to be around people who understand and support your religious beliefs.

When you make the commitment to carry a firearm for self-defense, you are putting the power of life and death within hand's reach. Treat that firearm with the respect it deserves. For today may be the day that death calls you and you must answer. Too often, we live in fear of death.

We should not fear death, but instead we should fear not living until death. Put first things first in your life. Remember, you can't take any of it with you in the end. We all die, and so it doesn't really matter how much you accomplish or how many possessions you accrue. What matters most is the amount of joy you spread, gratitude you exude and love you cultivate.

> Make peace with yourself
> Make peace with your family
> Make peace with God

Live more consciously each day. Stop sleepwalking through life. Your life is something to be experienced, not coasted through. Escape your ego. Began to see through new eyes. Began a new-found life with friends and a new-found love with your family and within your marriage. Once you have your life in order then you are able to commit fully in battle. Without hesitation you move, without fear you engage, and without remorse you are victorious. In this moment you don't think twice, there is no need to. You are at peace with yourself and your life. You express your feelings to those you need to, and you have your religious beliefs in order so that should you meet your death on the field of battle you are ready.

If I die then I die a free man who loved and lived a wholesome life with no regrets. Those that I leave behind should remember the many things that my life stood for and how I LIVED instead of merely existing. Each day I that I rise I live that day to the fullest. I pray that when I die, it is in the act of protecting innocence and that through my death, innocence continues to live.

Living without regret, sacrificing your life so that others may live…that is a hero's death. We can only hope that our own death will be worthy of such.

—EJ Owens

As I close this chapter, let me share with you this powerful speech that is as much about celebrating life, crossing over, and meeting your maker, as it is about facing the inevitable death of our mortal bodies with grace.

*"So live your life that the fear of death can never enter your heart.*

*Trouble no one about their religion; respect others in their view, and demand that they respect yours.*

*Love your life, perfect your life, beautify all things in your life.*

*Seek to make your life long and its purpose in the service of your people.*

*Prepare a noble death song for the day when you go over the great divide.*

*Always give a word or a sign of salute when meeting or passing a friend, even a stranger, when in a lonely place.*

*Show respect to all people and grovel to none.*

*When you arise in the morning give thanks for the food and for the joy of living.*

*If you see no reason for giving thanks, the fault lies only in yourself.*

*Abuse no one and no thing, for abuse turns the wise ones to fools and robs the spirit of its vision.*

*When it comes your time to die, be not like those whose hearts are filled with the fear of death, so that when their time comes they weep and pray for a little more time to live their lives over again in a different way.*

*Sing your death song and die like a hero going home."*

*—Tecumseh (1768-1813)*
*Native American leader, Shawnee*

Then said he unto them, But now, he that hath a purse, let him take it, and likewise his scrip: and he that hath no sword, let him sell his garment, and buy one.

—Luke 22:36 (KJV)

# 9

# LEGACY

Definition:

**leg·a·cy\ˈle-gə-sē\**

*noun*

: something (such as property or money) that is received from someone who has died
: something that happened in the past or that comes from someone in the past
: something transmitted by or received from an ancestor or predecessor or from the past

I FEEL LIKE the sun is just rising in my life and these are the years where I will define how I will go forward. I want to look back on this time and be proud of the person I'm becoming. During these next years, my devotion is set on living a life worth defending. Loving unconditionally, living life to the fullest, expressing my love for my family and living with honor is what I strive to achieve. I'll live out the rest of my time not wasting it on chasing frivolous personal desires, instead looking for ways to be a positive influence by bringing meaning and purpose to everything that I do. The story I want to have written about me is one of strength, faith, and laughter. These days seem to be long but the years are surely getting shorter. I want to know that the choices that I've made won't leave me wishing that I could make them again. My legacy will be written after I'm gone, as will yours. It will be defined by the influence and memories we have left behind.

For me, I carry a firearm for personal protection so that I might continue to live, fulfilling my true purpose here. I train to be the very best I can be so should the encounter happen I have the most advantage possible in order to walk away still breathing. As a man of faith, I believe that helping my fellow man is right and just in the eyes of God. I want to exceed my life goals and slide into my grave kicking, screaming, and exhausted because I gave all that I could to make myself, my family, and my friends better people than before I met them. I want my children to remember what I contributed to their upbringing and hold true to the principles of faith, family, and freedom. It is a difficult path, however, scathed with pitfalls of personal desires and character flaws. I haven't always been the man I would be proud to be. I haven't always said the right thing, acted the right way, and, in some cases, haven't been the bigger man and walked away. Funny how experience, not necessarily age, provides insight and meaning to our decisions.

What do you want your legacy to be? If you are not on the path to living like you have wanted then today you can wipe your slate clean and start anew. We all fall short for ourselves and others and we certainly can make a new beginning. It might be tough but you are stronger than you know. You have to believe me on this one because I am living proof that it can happen. You have to turn and face the clouds to see the silver lining. I've seen broken hearts become brand new and silent prayers answered. As a man of faith, I believe that impossible is not a word but a reason for someone not to try. Life is so much more than what your eyes are seeing and I promise you will find your way if you stay true to your purpose and have faith.

Faith is belief through action.

This world is constantly telling you how you can't... but you can! I have ups and downs in my life and have more to come, but I rest easy at night because I am doing everything that I can to be the man that I need to be. I strive to be the father my children need, preparing them to enter society and all that it holds. I am trying to be the husband that my wife is proud to hold hands with. I work at being the friend that I would like to have. I am still a work in progress and thankfully I have surrounded myself with mentors and close friends who continue to support and guide me.

I have had the pleasure of being my oldest son's baseball coach for the past eight years. He is fourteen now and pretty much an emancipated man in his mind and can make it on his own. However, during the last eight years together, we have seen both triumph and defeat on the baseball field. Many times I have called time-out to take the long trip to the mound in order to impart words of wisdom to him only to be met with some sort of shoulder shrug or head nod, both exhibiting lack of enthusiasm. I will tell you that he has not always agreed with me or my positive outlook on the severity of the current situation, and even more than that welcomed my suggestions on arm slot, bending more of the back, and follow-through, but what I can tell you is that there has never been a doubt in his mind that I was right there with him.

As with most children we often guide their decision-making process but ultimately it is their own decision to make. Nevertheless, we are there for them through the good and the bad times. The legacy that he will be left from me is simple: No matter what, Dad was there. I'll be honest with you, there are times when I want to just yank him off of that field and drag him into that dugout to rip him a new one for being so childish and immature (don't act like I'm the only parent who thinks of this stuff), but what I end up doing is pointing out where he could have made better decisions and had a more positive impact on his teammates by displaying leadership in the face of their hardship. He is still young and probably won't realize this till I'm dead and gone, but one day he *will* realize it. All of the players on the team benefit from the example of their coaches. They see how the coaches deal with the wide array of issues that arise during the game. They develop learned responses based on example. We often say, "It's not whether you win or lose, but how you play the game." I would ask you, "Is that any different than life?"

It's been my honor to sit on a bucket outside the dugout next to a great head coach and mentor to my son and the kids on our team. I have sat next to Brad Kornegay for the past five years and watched as he has demonstrated life lessons through the great game of baseball for over two hundred games. I have learned so much about how we approach life in general just by listening to him explain to these boys what we can learn through success and failure. The Army has taught me many things about leading men into battle, but Brad has taught me about growing boys into men. He has often told me, "Watch how you say it," "Tell them how it *can* be done," and more than I wanted to hear, "Let them go, they need to learn it themselves." I want to jump in and make it right. I want to tell them how not to make that mistake again. Brad has reminded me that it's okay to let them make mistakes while you are here to pick them up so hopefully they won't make them when you're gone.

Brad is very passionate about growing leaders. Leaders are the ones who get you through troubled times. In order to lead through troubled times, you first have to experience them yourself. It's through your own struggles and perseverance that you can empathize with, relate to, and ultimately motivate those who you will eventually lead.

Brad has a team saying that we say every time we take the field. He says, "I Believe," and the team echoes back, "God, Team, Me!" The methodology is simple yet concise.

**God:**
Through God, all things are possible.

**Team:**
No one person is greater than the team, it takes a team to lose or win the game.

**Me:**
I can be anything I want to be, do anything I want do in life, as long as I am willing to believe in myself, work harder, and never quit.

He is establishing life anchor points for these boys to grab onto when the real world starts to deal its hand to them. "Whenever something is not going right in your life," he says, "it's because you got your priorities out of order."

These pivotal life lessons will be a part of his legacy long after his time on Earth is over as what he has imparted is sure to remain for generations to come. What are you doing to impart a legacy to your family and friends? You may not have a team of athletes in a dugout like Brad does, but you do have people that you influence. Your team could be your family, your coworkers, or your close friends. As a protector and as a leader, you can directly impact your legacy by giving of yourself to others to aid them in being better family members, friends, parents, and even leaders.

Life is a succession of lessons which must be lived to be understood.

—Ralph Waldo Emerson

# 10

# COMPLETE

WE ARE ONLY here for a short time. During that time, three things will measure your existence: influence, example, and memories, the greatest being example. Live your life as an example in the pursuit of excellence. Live a life of love and laughter that is envious of others. It is constant work that requires you to change for the better what you can and accept that which you cannot.

Change begins first with you. Start with yourself. Look inward at your own pain. Can you forgive others? Do you need forgiveness? I do! I have wronged others and have been wronged. I have come to a point in my life where I won't be burdened by them and will travel outside of my comfort zone to forgive those that I thought I could never forgive. Conversely, I have had to seek forgiveness. I didn't always get it, but I am okay with it now because I have forgiven myself. You cannot expect everyone to be at a point in his or her life that you are at. All you can do is extend the hand of forgiveness and accept what comes of it. Prepare your soul to receive and extend forgiveness. I take time each day to give thanks for what I do have. I give thanks for the relationships I have been granted, the influence I have over my children, my wife, my family, and my friends. I am thankful for the trust they have in me and guard it as a great responsibility and honor to be a positive influence in their lives. Maybe something they see me do will impact them to defeat a fear and to take a chance at greatness despite their own doubts. That influence lives in you too! Don't let your example be tainted because of your own selfish desires.

We like to think of self-defense as a single act that denies the bad guy from taking your life away prematurely. I beg to differ. Self-defense is not just an act of counterviolence, but in addition, multiple acts, attitudes, and influence combining in our everyday encounters to further our positive existence while we are here. We defend our minds from evil thoughts, we guard our hearts from hardening, we protect the example of a moral right, and ultimately fortify a positive influence for that of being our brother's keeper. Living a life worth defending is to live a life of worth. Don't let another breath leave your body before you commit to impacting others with positive attributes that can aid them in having a better life.

Along the path to where you are now, you have had others give to you their time, effort, energy, and passion. They have helped to mold your character, your moral and ethical value system, and modeled for you how to express your love for others. Now is the time to pass along those to others. In here lies the greatest self-defense measures and security that you can give while you are here. For these are gifts that carry throughout one's life. Your example will show others how to defend their hearts, mind, and soul. You may never draw your gun in defense, but your life is in play everyday for all to see. Your life, a life worth defending, is defined by how you live.

So go to the ball games, take your daughter to ballet, and turn the music up loud as you dance with your wife in the kitchen. Go see your family more than on just the holidays. Kiss all your children everyday and tell them how much they mean to you. Hang up their drawings at your desk at work. Smile as your uncle tells his same ole tired joke that he has told you a million times. Brother, these are the things that you will remember as you meet your end, and I can tell you these are the things that your loved ones will remember about you. You are one of a kind, special in too many ways to explain. Let your example be the guiding light you leave behind for others to follow.

Tomorrow, wake up to the sunlight with an open heart. Don't hold in your anger and leave things unspoken. Let it all out and leave it out on the table, you won't regret it. Don't run from the truth because you can't get away. Face it head on and make right with yourself and others. Make peace with your family and God. Only then can you truly impact others for lasting goodness. The time is now. Pray for others even when you are hurting and think that you can't. Push yourself outside your comfort zone and when you look back from where you have been, you will be so much happier. Living a life worth defending starts with living.

The reason we train so hard and diligently is to pre-serve our life here on Earth, so until that time comes when you must defend it...

LIVE LIFE AND LIVE IT TO ITS FULLEST!

May God bless you and your family and may he continue to make your path straight and narrow. Pray for me and my continued walk as I am praying for you. Before I wrote these final words, I sat quietly and prayed for your life. God bless you, my warrior brethren!

It is not death that man should fear, but he should fear never beginning to live.

—Marcus Aurelius

# CLOSING

MANY THINK THAT a book on self-defense should be riddled with fighting positions, shooting stances, and techniques for disarming bad guys. I differ from that line of thinking in that one should live a life worth defending first. We will all die. Through our training we can shape how we greet death, whether it be naturally or in the throes of battle.

Fear not death and its impending arrival. You must realize that fear is not real. It is a product of thoughts you create. Do not misunderstand me, the danger is very real, but fear is a choice. I can only imagine when my day comes how I will smile at death knowing that my physical being will be removed but my influence, memories, and example will live on in others.

Others will be better and live more abundantly than I did simply because I made the choice to live a life worth defending. Weep not for me because I am no longer here but instead rejoice for the life that I have lived. I rejoice for you in the here and now, and should I leave you first,

I pray that I will meet you at the gates of heaven and rejoice for our reunion.

You are blessed beyond measure, but you—and only you—determine what you will do with those blessings.

*May God bless and protect you!*

# ABOUT THE AUTHOR

**EJ Owens is** a professional firearms instructor and an active Department of Defense Contractor. He is a Close Quarters Battle (CQB) Instructor and a U.S. Army Hand-to-Hand Combat Instructor. As a former Infantry Officer he is a veteran of the U.S. Army and National Guard. He is a Certified Glock Armorer, former firefighter and NREMT-P Paramedic with a specialty in Nuclear – Bio – Chemical Response, Rope Rappel Master, and a Competitive IDPA Shooter. He has a M.B.A. and is the President of Legally Concealed. EJ currently lives in Memphis, TN with his wife Jennifer and his three children Kaleb, Olivia, & Ethan.

Please check out EJ's other projects:

VIDEOS
**TACTICAL HOME DEFENSE**
**EVERYDAY CARRY**
**ESSENTIALS OF GUNFIGHTING**
**SO YOU BOUGHT AN AR**

BOOKS
**COUNTERVIOLENCE**
**A LIFE WORTH DEFENDING**

LIVE TRAINING
**MODERN WARRIOR**

MONTHLY SUBSRIPTION
**SHEEPDOG SOCIETY**

These and other products can be purchased at www.
legallyconcealed.org

Stay Alert and Practice Often! ™